Open Field

Open Field

Joseph Noto

Foreword by B. John Gully

RESOURCE *Publications* • Eugene, Oregon

OPEN FIELD

Resource Publications
An Imprint of Wipf and Stock Publishers
199 W. 8th Ave., Suite 3
Eugene, OR 97401

www.wipfandstock.com

PAPERBACK ISBN: 978-1-6667-6049-1
HARDCOVER ISBN: 978-1-6667-6050-7
EBOOK ISBN: 978-1-6667-6051-4

10/12/22

Contents

CONTENTS

Foreword: Life is

My friend, j.n., is a writer who has always had a keen sense of what death is. He told it to me in verse, told it in the very first poem he sent to me. Those words he arranged like colorful brushstrokes on a white canvas were pulled up from the very core of life itself. And at the core of life is death. To turn towards death, to dig at that core, is a brave thing—not for its chance of success but for its absolute futility.

Time has passed, quickly and slowly. It has shown me that those words my friend sent years ago were not isolated in their existence, but the beginning of his greater thesis that would face down the nature of futility. At Emerson College among the cycling autumns of the world, the words of this collection you hold have been arranged onto another canvas. They stand to show all who look on them what it means to turn towards death and life simultaneously.

The piece that gives this collection its name is number 18: *open field*. As I read this poem, I was struck by a feeling both familiar and fleeting. It comes back to me in dreams, and is recorded in my journal whenever it shows its face. And yet, it remains so elusive. It's something anticipatory, yet patient. It's sitting in the open fields of the world and feeling at one with our friendships, pain, yearning, and sickness.

j.n. writes of god, lifelessness, and the maddening nature of being alive. He writes of trying to face down the horrors life entails. He pulls from the work of another radically humanistic poet, Bukowski, whose gravestone is famously inscribed with the words "don't try." Don't try to get rich. Don't try to create. Don't try not to die. Numbers 38 and 39, which close this collection, tell their own story of what has had to occur in order for all of the other poems to exist: fear and feeling. 38 describes fear and ends with a first step. 39 describes what writing is, and ends with discovered beauty. My friend invites you to follow a first step into the jagged steps that follow towards life and death. I invite you to do the same in the pages that follow.

Let this collection show you what life is: turning towards death, and turning away from it. Not trying, but being. Let it sit with you in the open fields as you linger in spite of the fear within you.

B. John Gully
10:32 AM
6/12/2022

dear god

there they were, the
eyes of god staring
at me point blank.
i couldn't help the
way i looked
back at them,
eyes sitting lifeless,

the well

drink from the well
of your self
and begin
again."—charles Bukowski

sitting cross-legged by
rounded limestone,
a thousand feet deep.
sapphire water, oak pail;
porcelain tumbler before you.

start from page one;
a new book entirely—

the leaves turn, turn, turn
bringing you back to life,
filling you with breath.

drink—

sip after considerate sip,
trickling down the throat;

splash your face, let it
soak into your pores

drink,
then drink some more

two roads

two roads.
two diverging
paths.
they twist

intertwine
then diverge again.
back and forth,
two roads.
split the difference.
split the distance.
split the hairs standing on end.
split an atom like a cherry tomato.

split it all down the middle.
have them move in parallel.
no longer allow them to
intertwine, diverge
at their own will.
two roads.
two diverging
roads.
split the sun.
split the clouds.

split a blade of grass.

split a molecule.

split the universe.

split the milky way galaxy in half.

split a dwarf planet like a lime.

split the stardust in Your eyes.

two roads.

every day you wake up

and it's the same.

the clock tick,

        tick,

           ticks,

               and You repeat.

everything is just the

        same shade of grey.

tick,

    tick,

        tick,

tick.

two roads.

i wish you could

        understand how this feels.

to be torn apart

        at the seams.

split my head.

split the frontal lobe.

split the smallest neuron.

split a synapse in motion.

two roads.

i guess in some ways

        you're still that six-year-old boy.

sitting at the bottom

        of the pool gasping for air.

nothing has really

        changed at all, has it?

two roads.

let's talk about death

let's talk about death.

let's talk about all the things you hid,
about the dark crevices.

let's talk about the cold end,
about the hole in your chest.

let's talk about everything that makes you anxious,
about all the things you fear.

let's talk about all the roaches in the ashtray,
about all the shattered glass.

let's talk about that rope in your garage,
about the burgundy splattered on the bedsheet.

let's talk about what makes your blood boil.

let's talk about how our eye faded.

anchor

my heart is the anchor,
your body is the vessel,
together we navigate the sea
coursing the tempestuous winds
catching them in the sails
traversing the world.

an ocean glazed world,
we set down the anchor
allowing rest for the vessel;
the calming nature of the sea,
cool breeze of the winds
wishing to catch one of our sails.

the flapping of the sails;
the whisper of the world.
we hoist the anchor
and get to moving the vessel;
waves course through the sea
and there are brave, roaring winds.

we cast away with the winds
getting caught in the sails.
we want to see the world;

we can't be held down by an anchor.
the restlessness of the vessel
skating on top of the sea.

the waters of the sea
match the tempo of the winds;
there's a rough patch in the sails
and a rough patch in the world.
my heart can't always be the anchor
that drags down your vessel.

you've got a strong vessel;
strong enough for this blazing sea,
strong enough to contain the winds
strength in each of the sails,
strength of the whole world;
strong enough to fight the anchor

the winds are caught in the sails,
the world is our sea;
your body the vessel, my heart the anchor.

refraction

the world
refracts, shatters,
then becomes whole
again. it's a
vicious
cycle.
i'm caught
in the loop
of staring at
screens
of different shapes
and sizes for
days on end.
i exhale
dandelions
just to pass
the time.
i am
one with the
earth.
i lie in
the grass and
soak up the rich
soil.

i am

one with the

universe.

i fall into

the cosmic worm

hole

and i am

absent

again.

tick,

tick,

tick.

where did the

day go?

another day

lost

in the

spacetime

vortex.

life is just

a gradual

decay.

the diminishing

of what you

once held
near and
dear to your
heart.
life seems to
be, to me
at least,
the never-ending
sacrifice to
one's own
hopes and
dreams.
how did you
let them all
unravel?
every sacrifice taking a
chip away.
your paper-skin
is burning at
the edges.
you're burning
the candle at
both ends again.
midnight

stalker and
early morning
creeper.
rise and shine,
sunshine.
it's 7
a.m.
wasn't it just
3? well,
here we go.
it's all a
cosmic gumbo
of shades of grey,
culminating in
a droopy
mess on the
plate.

autumn

and just as
the leaves
change,
so do
i.
from green to
yellow,
orange,
red,
brown,
they all
change.
just as
the leaves
change
in autumn,
so do
i.
i am
ever-changing.
and
just as
the leaves
change,

so do
you.
you
learn and
you
expand.
the roots are
watered and
new sprouts
blossom.
just as
in autumn,
you go through
a transformation,
perhaps an
evolution.
and
just as
autumn
leaves,
you leave.
as time moves
and the
seasons

change,
you go
with it.
autumn
to winter,
and you
move
to colder states.
the autumnal
equinox
has come and
gone,
you left
me
staring through the
wall
again.
left hands
empty grasping
air turning
into
clenched
fists.
just as

autumn
leaves,
you leave.
then,
i leave.
i move to
different
galaxies,
i can never
stay in one
place.
andromeda,
the large
magellanic cloud,
the triangulum,
i visit them all.
and just as
autumn
leaves,
i leave.
autumn moves to
winter
and i
move to

colder states
of being.
the
vagabond
on a road
searching for,
searching for the
truth.
i enter this
journey
so i
alone
can be the
honored one.
and just as
my cup
runneth
over,
it is soon
empty,
lost to
spillage
and drink.
searching for

something more
in the stars,
and searching for
deeper roots
in the ground.
under the
heavens,
above the
heavens,
i yearn to be
the unrivaled one,
all alone.
and just as
autumn
leaves,
i leave.

summer heat

amber august
sunshine
suicide.

brother

perhaps in words only,
but a brother nonetheless.
perhaps not related through blood,
but two souls forged
through time. i was born into the
world alone, but somewhere along
the way i found you.

perhaps a brother in words only,
but one nonetheless.
my guide, protector,
best friend.
there is no one else in this world
who could be a
substitute. not bonded by
blood but through
intertwining of
minds and souls.

i wish there were
enough words in any
language to describe how
i feel about you.

unfortunately, words alone
could never do justice
to what you mean to me.

perhaps a brother in words only,
but a brother nonetheless.
brother, hear my words
through the page—

feel them in your heart,
know my love rings true.

remember all the wholesome—
the wicked,
the sufferings,
the smiles.

all the 4 a.m. conversations,
the drives with the windows
down and the music blasting,
all the times you warned me
not to do *this* or *that*.
the rift

that *she* almost caused, but our
perseverance prevailed.
your wisdom, wise beyond
your years, something I'd be lost without.
late nights pondering different meanings
of all different things and sometimes
finding no answers.
commiserating for one another in
the front seats of cars.
sighing together, crying together,
even the promise of dying together.

a brother in words only,
but one nonetheless.
times spent extinguishing dandelions and
devouring vapors.
times spent couch locked in another dimension.
times spent feeling the breeze in our lungs.
times i'd never give back—
times i'll cherish forever.

do you hate people?

My demons love to visit,
they take the time out of
their day to stop in, check
on me, make sure I'm
doing alright. Aren't they
so kind? To tell the truth,
I feel better when they're
not around. I tell them to
stop coming by but they
must be hard of hearing
because they keep on
showing up, unannounced.

I don't hate them, I don't
hate anyone or any thing. . .
I feel better when I'm alone,
sometimes, at least. . .
I guess I shouldn't get too
angry, they're just trying to
keep me company, but presence
brings pain—pain leaves
scars on paper skin—paper
skin disintegrates and scars
fade from existence. . .a new

layer for new scars, and it all
repeats. *I don't hate them. . .*
I don't hate them. . .I
don't hate them. . .I don't
hate them. . .I don't hate
them. . .I don't hate them.

an allegory

i am still only three
or four with duct tape
across my lips and
my arms tied behind
my back and my ank
-les bound and i was
bawling my eyes out
while those monsters
took their medieval
instrument to her stom
-ach and i was screaming
bloody murder through
the duct tape but no
one cared no one did
a thing to stop those
monsters and i stood
there and bawled my
eyes out because they
had her lied out on the
bed arms and legs spra
-wled and they had this
sharp metal instrument
that my father used for
work and i didn't know

what was going on but
my body was shaking
quivering from head to
toe and the fear of mon
-sters trying to hurt my loved
ones with myself being power
-less against them never went
away because i am still
small and i am still weak
and i am nothing but a
cosmic speck in a massive
playing field of nothingness
and i am powerless against
monsters and i am power
-less against god and
i am
powerless against myself
and i don't know what's
going on but i know
that i am still scared.

storm

there is a
storm
raging inside of
me.
the
tempestuous winds
roaring in my
lungs.
inhale,
exhale the
eye
of the
storm.
the lightning
strikes
my alveoli
and i'm
renewed
again.
thunder claps
as bellowing
glass coughs
concave my
chest cavity.

there is a
ripple
in the ocean.
the waves course
like a tsunami
devastating the
ventricles and
atriums of my heart.
the capillaries
flood and my
eyes burst into
waterworks.

associated

my grandfather knew a lot of people and he
worked at the airport for a long time. people would
come visit him and ask numerous questions about
his line of work and all the people that he knew.
what family are you in? the noto family.
who's that? me, my wife, my son, and my daughter. i
had heard this story countless times throughout my years
growing up in that house. i heard plenty about
the warehouse too, shit i was even in it,
there are pictures of it somewhere in dusty old
books hidden under a bed in a room somewhere
in the house. that's what it was like to be
associated with a certain *kind of people.*
you get harassed, you get your door beaten down, you
get all kinds of looks, but you also get treated
a certain way by others. some people will kiss
the ring on your hand and bow their head to you, some
will give you the fanciest of meals gratis, some
will call you things like don and you'll need to clarify
that you're not associated, *no, you're don, well,*
shit. they all seemed like they could be fairytales in
my younger years and maybe that's why my grandfather
was always my knight in shining armor until
his last breath. even now, his prayer card sits above

the fireplace in this very room and watches
over me, keeping me honest and protected.
he told me all about snake-eyes and showed me all
the glistening gold, the diamonds and rubies and
sapphires. he showed me that his stories weren't
fairytales, that they were lived. that he really did
let those people in during the middle of the
night and gave them plates of food. that he really did
get saved in cuba because he dropped his cigarette
and bent down to pick it up. that he really did
stay at all the finest places and had the most
magnificent rides and that he was living in
style. i would have liked to see it, but i'm happier
than i ever could be with what i got. i had
a grandfather who could fill my mind with wonder
and amazement, who never once let me down. a
grandfather who imparted everything he had
in me. a grandfather who at times was batted
down by life, but never once thought about quitting.
a grandfather who was associated so
he got the blunt end of the stick sometimes. a man
who i could idolize, something to strive towards. a
grandfather who loved deeply and taught me just the same.

words

my words
bleed off
the page—

spill over onto
the desk and
stain it crimson.

the words
bead up and
roll off my lips,

dribble down my
chin and drivel
onwards.

i'm incoherent;
minds a
filthy mess—

reminiscent of
bedroom corners
crawling with old

laundry and empty
containers, the filth
piles up in every space.

liquid dreams
with such
lucidity,

but i can't
transfigure
it into legible

writing or phrase.
i am at a loss.
i am losing.

block

grind your
teeth

—grit—

won't last
too
l o n g.

seamless
time

fluttering—

fairies of
the unseelie
court blitz
by my brow.

where

did you
go?

where?

why?
always like
this. . .

yearning

i yearn for
your call—

reach out
and grab me,

caress me with
your gentle words.

tell me all the
lies i crave to hear.

tell me all the
hard truths i'm
not ready for,

hushed murmurs
beating my eardrum.

you always beat
simmering silence.

let your words
trickle down the ear canal.

drip them down
until they reach the bottom—

tickle my mind,
a little foreplay never hurt.

subtle fits
of ubiquitous
consciousness.

thought stimulation,
i've been looking for that
sensation—

sinful bliss,
laced behind your lips.

gone

ice-struck bones—

my veins pump antifreeze.

i shutter by your gravestone,
sitting cross-legged in front of marble.

placing rocks atop it.

you left, but the
memories linger.

treasures—

greater than a chest
filled with beautiful gemstones.

coffee tears lain over
a chestnut casket.

your pain is
gone now,

no longer aching.

like autumn, you've left
a trail of leaves behind,

but nothing can
shake this cold.

open field

waking up to morning dew
lain down in the field,
i watch the rising sun,
feel the cool of the breeze,
all the radiant flowers;
look—a dangling spider.

it crawls on a limb, the spider
illuminated by the righteous sun,
hands brush off morning dew
scurry through the field
surrounded by magnificent flowers,
in the slow wake of the breeze.

here comes the morning's breeze
again, delicate as flowers.
everything ignited by the sun
as the looming spider
reaches the grassblades soaked in dew
cast away in the open field.

what if the world were my field
and i were the spider
or maybe i were the flowers

soaked in fresh dew
glowing in the breeze,
glazed by the sun.

the morning glory of the sun,
the flash of breeze.
wood touches dew
sprawled in the spacious field,
and the capricious spider
climbing atop the flowers.

line my casket with flowers
in divine rays of the sun
as one crawling spider
floats in the breeze
riding on the field
tasting morning dew.

the spider rules the field
stealing morning dew in the breeze
as the sun brightens my bed of flowers.

dance

autumn leaves twirl and dance
through the peaceful skies,
cotton candy clouds above and
black tar pavement below, yet these
leaves hover in between looking for a
home to call their own because the
only home they have ever known
let them fall and drift through the
open air on their own, lonesome,
the parental tree pushing the
leaves from their branches telling
them it is their time to float on,
but these leaves are dead inside,
they've dried out, veins become rigid,
nothing courses through them anymore,
everything has left in one way or another,
lost in time and drifting through the space,
they're on their own journey now, this might be
the end, or simply the beginning, destiny is
uncertain, but the leaves journey
through their afterlife, looking to reach the heavens.

what a circus!

flame-eater,
sword
swallower,
what a circus!

we are all going
to die, but that
doesn't seem to
be enough to
spread love for
one another. so
stuck on the
minute, soon to
be swallowed
whole.
we look like
sustenance.

slow burn

burning my fingertips—
the gradual blister beginning
to take shape, oval-ish,
let it harden and callus over;

i've taken to smoking
cigarettes again and the
stench permeates through
every article of clothing,
my long, dark chocolate hair.

my throat stings so
blissfully, smoke them
so short you could call
the butts stingers—

i've got a glass
cough that just won't
quit; bellowing
glass coughs
through the corridor. . .

my alveoli are
tar and resin
and my bronchioles
are carved by
fiberglass.

i can feel the build up
in my trachea, hack up
another lung, let it all out.

breathe

inhale,
exhale.
watch as the
trees breathe,
wavering in the
fresh air,
taking in all my
carbon dioxide
and returning it
back to oxygen.

inhale,
exhale.
no longer sipping
on fresh air but
gulping down
carcinogens—

close your eyes,
count each breath.

open them now
and watch the
leaves on their
descent to
the ground.

twisting and
twirling through
air like a
ballet dancer.

the autumnal
equinox has
come and gone,
but the reds and
yellows linger;
they dance so tenderly,
having trained a
lifetime for
this moment.

red line

a train's worth of
people meshed
with a train's worth
of people
and it's a frightful
dark;
time ticks on,
tests temptation.

pace

i think i'll give a name to my
pain, it only seems fair, after all
i have a name. what to call it?

maybe i'll call it default. . .

default, i say, do you want something
to drink? were you once a
roach? why don't you
sleep?
take a rest?
die?

default follows me across
the room, pacing along
my side.

sometimes i don't know if
i am me or default.

some say i revel in it.

yes, i jump for joy
clasping default's hands until
my soles bleed.

the mind is blank

for a moment
I forget about myself
forget about the sun
the blazing heat
the stars
their dying light
the earth
the moving mountains
the universe
time freezes with a
stone chill and the
world stops rotating
its orbit stops
everything stops
I stop and the
mind forgets about
knowing because to
know is to hurt.

on serenity

a grey fitted
sheet and a
concrete blanket

sink me into the
bed frame.

sometimes i
ogle the
tracks, they
could be
a mattress—

sometimes bridges
look like diving
boards,

knots are a
daisy chain.

life can be
magenta
amber
but right now it's
asphalt.

so cozy here
spilling
scarlet—

even the devil has company, you know?

i've heard that it's
lonely at the top,
but i can't imagine
myself taking in that
view. i'm meant for the
gutters; lord of the
slums and keeper of
the decrepit.

tempest

caught in a flaming storm,
a whirlwind of sadness—
he was just a boy at the time,
struggling to discover something divine. . .
searching deep within
to find a well of truth.

to tell the truth
he was the tempest's storm.
waves crash like sadness
while trying to murder time—
he prayed the "our father" to the divine
staying on the path within.

he was stuck within
a land of friction. the search for the truth
halted by a violent snow storm—
buried by his own sadness
lead to a culmination of wasted time.
there is nothing as splendid as the divine

and he was spoiled by the divine;
during his journey within
he became lost. the hidden truth

whipping up like a hellish storm,
struck by lightning sadness
at the worst time.

spending days at a time
wishing upon the divine.
walking on the road within
he stumbled upon a whittled truth.
as he's engulfed by the storm
there is a thunderclap of sadness

and he drowns in a sea of sadness
while counting out time—
looking for a way out through the divine.
he strolls down the passage within
until he reaches the truth.
one day he will realize that he is the storm

because the storm is him, it fills him with brittle sadness—
he found the way to murder time while waiting on the divine.
he walked the whole trail within and found his solemn truth.

eminence

a beautiful
blackish eminence.
be gentle fair maiden for my
tender skin bruises easily, as does
my heart. be gentle as we make
night moves; gentle, gentle into
that hollow night. fair maiden,
be careful with my soul, easily
fractured. i give to thee my
beating heart to hold in the
palm of your hands.

how much a dollar cost?

pockets empty;
wasteland
in the palm of my
hand. "i'm not
dangerous and i'm
not begging, i'm not
a drug addict,"
i'm sorry but my
pockets are an oasis of
sand alone. there is no
water here to quench your
thirst. grit your teeth and
persevere in the quicksand.
don't let it drag you down
farther, it can easily
bury you. pockets
deserted; dollars flee
for safety. "can you spare
anything?" i wish i could,
but my wallet is hollow, only
plastic echoes, and even the
plastic is bare. god how i wish
i could help, but i can't even
help myself.

sick

my innards are
rancid, turned to
toxic sludge.
rotting from the
inside out, it
consumes me. it's
an illness, a cancer
that plagues me.
corrosive organs
wrapped up in
an eroding flesh
casing.

they're all out having fun

living it up, having a
ball while she sits at
home in bed pondering
de anima and if her
soul is composed of
flames or if she even
has a soul at all, maybe
it's just a bunch of make
believe and we are nothing
more than a sack of flesh
filled with liquid crimson,
maybe there is no higher
purpose and when it's all
over we end up in the dirt,
no transcendence for her,
not for anyone, but there's
always hope that her
innards are made of fire.

i can't write for shit

not last week,
not yesterday,
not today,
probably not
tomorrow.

my head is a
jumble, so messy
and cluttered. i
can't form a
coherent thought
to save my life—

yet i keep trying
to find something,
not entirely sure
what, but some
thing. please come
to me, ease this pain
in my head and the
hurt in my chest. . .

don't linger on the
trivial, don't linger
at all. "forward, move
forward," but i feel
sedentary. there's
desperation behind
these bloodshot eyes.
i'm hungry, but words
don't always feed
mouths. . .

i'm trailing, losing train of
thought; thoughts left
behind like mementos,
i hope you treasure them.
they're all that you will have
left of me.

weeds

the weeds are tangled
in his ventricles—ensnared is
his heart, surrounded by
rotting ribs and flimsy flesh.
the weeds are caught up in
his atriums, they slip out
through the aorta, the
pulmonary vein and artery,
they constrict the heart from
the inside out—the sternum is
decaying, the heart is restrained,
the body is deteriorating
rapidly, but the weeds still grow.

blowing your life up

inspired by graeme guttman

sometimes it starts with
skipping your meds or a
line of blow on a night
out— sometimes it's
smoking a blunt to the
face and forgetting who
you are for a while. other
times it's texting your
ex in the middle of the
night or picking up the
razor blade early in the
morning. often it's chewing
your cuticles off and biting
your lips until they bleed—
you see the people in the
park smiling and laughing,
happy, thriving, and you
know that you're never
going to be like them
because you love the
thrill of everything you
shouldn't have.

stuck in cycle

my life is stuck
in cycles like loads
of laundry. all the
clothes are dirty and
they need a proper
wash.

i've been going through
periods of either
sleeping too much or
not sleeping enough
and my eyes feel like
sandbags.

cement weighs heavy
on my soles and i'm
dragging my feet
through muck
turning the grey
to brown.

life is heavy
just as the cycles
are endless;
stuck in a stream
of consciousness
but it's wavering. . .

learning

he's still learning what
it means to live,
and it's a slow

lesson. there's
no set formula or
equation to bring

him to an exact
answer, on
occasion there is

a hint towards the
right direction.
But with every

step forward he
takes at least
five steps back;

he's losing track
of progress and
only focusing on

the set backs.
but he's still
trying every

day to push
onward and to
keep living.

what he does

he takes words and
puts them in a particular

order and calls it
art. he arranges them

to be pleasing yet
dreary. he would like

to be acknowledged
but his hands tremble

in fear. thinking that
his words aren't

good enough to
get noticed or to

get picked up by
a magazine or a

journal or an
editor at a

publishing house.
but that's just his

anxiety speaking, he
won't truly know

until he takes his
first step.

writing is

sinking her teeth into
the paper and taking a
hearty bite. it's putting
his fist through a wall
and never fixing the
hole or it's ceramic tears
dripping down the screen.
maybe it's petrified water
staining the edges. the
vomit he couldn't hold
back because he was too
anxious. sometimes it's
chewing her lips until they're
raw, and biting off living
skin from her fingers.
and sometimes it's looking into
her eyes and feeling the
ardor of being with her.

www.ingramcontent.com/pod-product-compliance
Lightning Source LLC
La Vergne TN
LVHW051707080426
835511LV00017B/2784